WILD WORK

WHO COUNTS THE PENGUINS?
WORKING IN ANTARCTICA

Mary Meinking

www.raintreepublishers.co.uk
Visit our website to find out
more information about
Raintree books.

To order:
☎ Phone 0845 6044371
🖹 Fax +44 (0) 1865 312263
📠 Email myorders@raintreepublishers.co.uk

Customers from outside the UK please telephone +44 1865 312262

Raintree is an imprint of Capstone Global Library Limited,
a company incorporated in England and Wales having its
registered office at 7 Pilgrim Street, London, EC4V 6LB –
Registered company number: 6695582

Text © Capstone Global Library Limited 2011
First published in hardback in 2011
Paperback edition first published in 2012
The moral rights of the proprietor have been asserted.

Edited by David Andrews, Nancy Dickmann, and Rebecca
Rissman
Designed by Victoria Allen
Picture research by Liz Alexander
Leveled by Marla Conn, with Read-Ability.
Originated by Dot Gradations Ltd
Printed and bound in China by Leo Paper Products

ISBN 978 1 4062 1683 7 (hardback)
15 14 13 12 11
10 9 8 7 6 5 4 3 2 1

ISBN 978 1 4062 1947 0 (paperback)
16 15 14 13 12
10 9 8 7 6 5 4 3 2 1

British Library Cataloguing in Publication Data
Meinking, Mary.
    Who counts the penguins? : working in Antarctica. --
(Wild work)
    1. Earth scientists--Antarctica--Juvenile literature.
    2. Biologists--Antarctica--Juvenile literature.
    3. Antarctica--Research--Juvenile literature.
    I. Title II. Series
    508.9'89-dc22

Acknowledgements
The author and publisher are grateful to the following for
permission to reproduce copyright material:
Alamy pp. **9** (© David Leatherdale), **25** (© Bubbles
Photolibrary), **26** (© tbkmedia.de), **27** (© Dan Leeth);
Bluegreenpictures.com P. **5** (© Ingo Arndt); British Antarctic
Survey p. **24** (Pete Bucktrout); Corbis pp. **10** (© Image Plan),
12 (© Ann Hawthorne), **17** (© Johannes Kroemer), **23**; Getty
Images pp. **4** (Cliff Leight/Aurora), **13** (Daisy Gilardini/The
Image Bank), **15** (National Geographic), **18** (DreamPictures/
Photographer's Choice), **19** (Keren Su/The Image Bank),
22 (Ralph Lee Hopkins/National Geographic), **28** (Torsten
Blackwood/AFP), **29** (Torsten Blackwood/AFP); Photolibrary
p. **7** (Mark Hannaford/John Warburton-Lee Photography);
Photoshot p. **11** (© NHPA); Science Photo Library pp. **14**
(George Steinmetz), **16** (British Antarctic Survey), **20** (Karim
Agabi/ Eurelios), **21** (Karim Agabi/ Eurelios); Shutterstock (©
alysta) **background images**; U.S. Air Force photo/Tech. Sgt.
Nick Przybyciel p.**8**.

Cover photograph reproduced with permission of iStockphoto
(© Alexander Hafemann).

Every effort has been made to contact copyright holders
of material reproduced in this book. Any omissions will
be rectified in subsequent printings if notice is given to
the publisher.

Contents

Frozen land

Welcome to Antarctica, the coldest place on Earth. Ice is everywhere. There's no sun in the winter. And you could get **frostbite** in the summer!

Thousands of people work here.
Scientists are always learning
new things in this frozen land.

The big chill

Antarctica is at the South Pole. It holds the record for the coldest **temperature** ever recorded: – 89.2°C (–128.6°F). The land is covered by ice that has been there for millions of years.

South Pole

SOUTHERN OCEAN

Antarctic Circle

0   500   1000 Miles
0   500   1000 Kilometres

South America

Antarctica

SOUTHERN OCEAN

SOUTHERN OCEAN

This is an Argentinian research base.

No country owns Antarctica. **Scientists** from around the world go there to study. Britain has four **research** bases there.

Prepare for landing

There are two ways to get to Antarctica—by air or sea. Large planes and ships bring the big stuff scientists need, such as equipment and building materials.

Smaller planes bring the people and their gear. Most planes have skis to land on the ice.

Pilots in planes and **helicopters** fly **scientists** around Antarctica. They have to keep their engines running. They might not start again if they are turned off. Fuel turns as thick as syrup when it gets that cold.

No one flies in the winter or when
the weather is bad. Pilots can't land
if they can't see the runway.

Smashing through ice

Big ships are needed to bring heavy things to Antarctica. The ships are built to be strong so they don't get damaged by the ice.

icebreaker ship

Some ships get to Antarctica too early or leave too late. They get stuck in the ice. Icebreaker ships cut a path to free the trapped ship.

Drilling through time

Glaciologists (say *glay-see-ol-oh-jists*) study Antarctica's ice. When new snow falls, it slowly packs the old snow into ice. Some of Antarctica's ice is about 5 kilometres (3 miles) thick!

The ice gives **scientists** clues about what was happening in the world when it froze. Glaciologists drill out long pieces of ice. These pieces of ice can show ancient snow falls and when volcanoes erupted.

Glaciologists can tell what the **climate**, or average weather, was like 800,000 years ago. Computers compare today's climate to climates in the past.

The Earth is getting warmer. Antarctica's ice is starting to melt. That cools the oceans. So everyone's weather is changing.

Counting heads

Biologists study animals, such as penguins, that live in freezing Antarctica. **Scientists** check if there are more or fewer of them each year.

In late winter and early spring, biologists count penguins. At that time only the males are there guarding their eggs. The females are off feeding. The scientists know there are twice as many penguins as they can see.

Star light, star bright

Astronomers say Antarctica is a perfect place to study stars. In the winter, Antarctica is one of the darkest places on Earth.

Even in summer, Antarctica is a great place for star gazing!

DID YOU KNOW?

A new **observatory** is being built in Antarctica. The star photos taken there will be better than any others taken from Earth.

Rock hunters

Geologists search for **fossils** in Antarctica. The fossils show Antarctica was warm millions of years ago.

fossil

meterorite

Antarctica is also the best place to find **meteorites**. These dark rocks from space are easy to spot against the white snow. **Scientists** have even found rocks from the Moon and Mars!

Help me doctor!

Everybody seems to do **research** in Antarctica. Some people even research the researchers! They study how Antarctica affects people in winter. This is a hard time. Not many people can come and go. The sun is down all day long. People work, eat, and sleep differently.

Sun lamps help
workers feel better.

Helping hands

Everyone in Antarctica has a job to do. Some people keep workers healthy. Others keep the bases running well.

These postal workers make sure everyone gets their post.

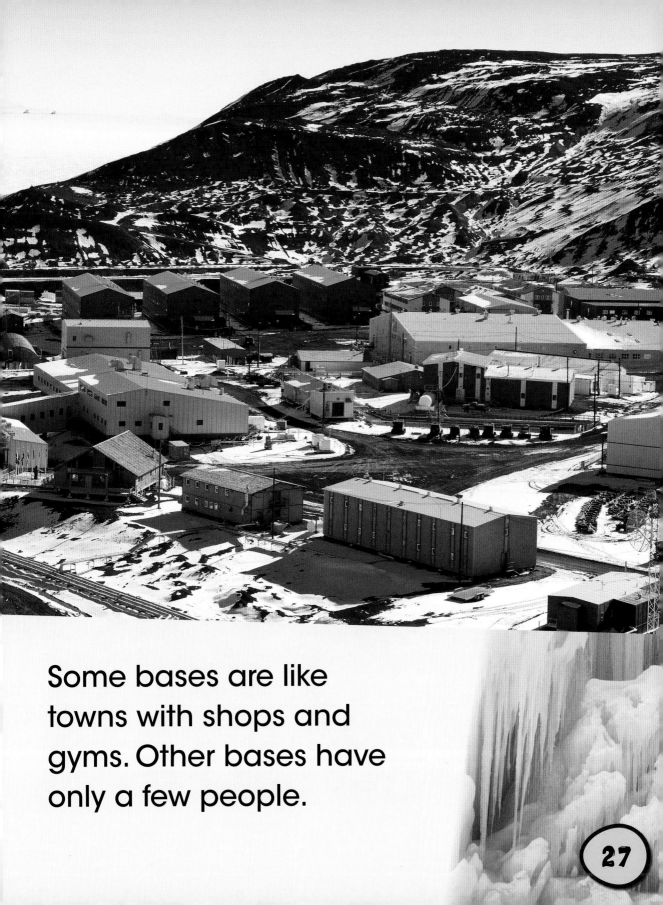

Some bases are like
towns with shops and
gyms. Other bases have
only a few people.

Could you work in Antarctica?

Many people want to work in Antarctica. They have to be healthy. They can't leave for emergencies.

Workers must love their jobs. They work 54 hours per week. Workers eat in canteens and don't have much space for themselves. But they say, "Once you work in Antarctica, you'll want to come back!"

Glossary

astronomer   scientist who studies objects in the sky

biologist   scientist who studies living things

climate   the average weather for a place

fossil   part of a living thing that has turned to stone

frostbite   injury to skin after being frozen

geologist   scientist who studies the Earth's surface, rocks, and minerals

glaciologist   scientist who studies snow and ice

helicopter   aircraft that's able to hover and can fly in any direction

meteorite   a stone that's fallen to Earth from space

observatory   building used to study objects in the sky

pilot   person who flies an aircraft

research   to search for the facts

scientist   an educated expert on one subject

temperature   how hot or cold something is

Find out more

Books to read

Antarctica, Lucy Bowman (Usborne, 2007)

Antarctica: Land of the Penguins, Angela and Jonathan Scott (Collins, 2005)

Exploring Antarctica, Tristan Boyer Binns (Raintree, 2007)

Websites

http://www.antarctica.ac.uk/living_and_working/index.php
Find out what life is like for researchers in Antarctica on the British Antarctic Survey website.

http://epa.gov/climatechange/kids/cc.html
Learn facts, play games, and find out what we can do to stop climate change.

http://icestories.exploratorium.edu/dispatches/
Polar scientists talk about the work they're doing in Antarctica.

http://www.teachers.tv/video/25202
Watch this video of British teachers on an expedition to Antarctica.

Index